Hot and Cold

Karen Bryant-Mole

Heinemann Interactive Library
Des Plaines, Illinois

First published in the United States by Heinemann Interactive Library,
an imprint of Reed Educational & Professional Publishing,
1350 East Touhy Avenue, Suite 240 West
Des Plaines, IL 60018

Customer Service 1-888-454-2279

Printed and bound in Hong Kong
Designed by Jean Wheeler
Commissioned photography by Zul Mukhida
Consultant—Hazel Grice

© BryantMole Books 1998

02 01 00 99
10 9 8 7 6 5 4 3 2

Library of Congress Cataloging-in-Publication Data
Bryant-Mole, Karen.
     Hot and cold / by Karen Bryant-Mole.
       p.   cm. -- (Science all around me)
     Includes bibliographical references and index.
     Summary: Text and experiments introduce the sceintific properties
of heat and cold, examining such topics as temperature,
thermometers, freezing, and melting.
       ISBN 1-57572-628-9 (library binding)
     1. Heat--Juvenile literature. 2. Heat--Experiments--Juvenile
literature. 3. Cold--Juvenile literature. 4. Cold--Experiments-
-Juvenile literature. [1. Heat. 2. Heat--Experiments. 3. Cold.
4. Cold--Experiments. 5. Experiments.] I. Title. II. Series.
QC256.B79   1998
536--dc21   97-41947
                                                       CIP
                                                       AC

A number of questions are posed in this book. They are designed to consolidate children's understanding by encouraging further exploration of the science in their everyday lives.

Acknowledgments
The Publishers would like to thank the following for permission to reproduce photographs: Eye Ubiquitous p. 20; James Davis p. 12; Positive Images p. 6; Tony Stone Images pp. 10, 18 (Lori Adamski Peek), p. 14 (Joel Bennett), p. 16 (Michael Rosenfeld), p. 22 (John and Eliza Forder), Zefa p. 4.

Every effort has been made to contact copyright holders of any material reproduced in this book. Any omissions will be rectified in subsequent printings if notice is given to the Publisher.

Words that appear in the text in bold can be found in the glossary.

Contents

Temperature

We use the words, "hot and "cold" to describe **temperature**.

The food that this waiter is carrying on his tray is cold.

? *Can you think of a food that is usually served hot?*

See for yourself...

Holly is eating her favorite meal. She is having pizza, followed by strawberries and cream.

The pizza is hot but the strawberries and cream are cold. Is your favorite food hot or cold?

Temperature Words

There are many words used to describe **temperature**.

The water in this swimming pool could be described as warm. Other temperature words include cool, **tepid,** and **lukewarm.**

? *Do you prefer swimming in warm water or cool water?*

See for yourself...

Brian and Jonathan are washing dishes.

Brian thinks the water is warm, but Jonathan thinks it is lukewarm.

Words like "hot," "warm," and "lukewarm" are useful but they don't tell us the exact temperature.

Measuring Temperature

To find out exactly how hot or cold something is, we have to **measure** its **temperature**.

Temperature is measured using a **thermometer**. A thermometer is being used to measure this girl's body temperature.

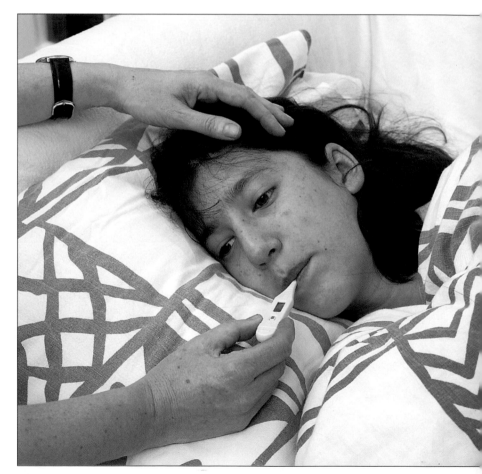

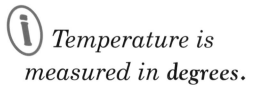 *Temperature is measured in degrees.*

See for yourself...

Jessica is using a room thermometer to measure the temperature of the air.

If the air temperature gets hotter, the red **liquid** inside the thermometer will rise up.

The number next to the top of the liquid shows Jessica the air temperature.

9

Feeling Temperature

We feel **temperature** through our skin.

The people in this picture are sitting in the sunshine.
They can feel the hot sun through the skin on their faces,
arms, and legs.

(i) *When you eat, you feel the temperature of the food through the skin inside your mouth.*

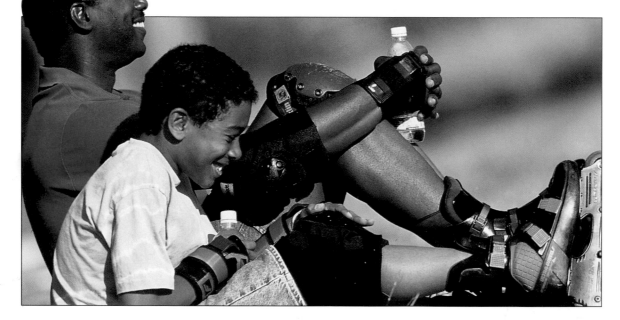

See for yourself...

Brian asked his mother to fill one bowl with warm water and another with cold water.

Brian can't tell them apart just by looking. But as soon as he tests the water with his finger, he can feel which is which.

Weather

Weather can feel hot or cold.

In winter, the air is colder than it is in summer. The cold air makes us feel cold. The hot air in summer makes us feel hot.

Which season do you prefer, summer or winter?

See for yourself...

We wear different types of clothes in hot and cold weather.

One of these children is wearing cold weather clothes. The other is wearing hot weather clothes.

Can you tell which is which?

13

Freezing

If **liquids** get cold enough, they will **freeze**.

This iceberg is made of frozen water. Ice cubes and hailstones are also made of frozen water.

The temperature at which something freezes is called its "freezing point."

See for yourself...

Holly wants to freeze some orange juice to make a popsicle.

She is pouring the juice into a clean plastic cup. She has pushed a clean popsicle stick through the lid.

When she puts the lid on, her father will freeze it in the freezer.

Melting

Heating things can make them **melt**.

The metal in this picture has been heated in a very hot fire called a furnace. Now it is so hot it has melted and can be poured.

Things that have melted are described as "molten."

See for yourself...

Jessica put some chocolate on a saucer.

She placed the saucer on a windowsill where the sun was shining.

After awhile she went back to the saucer.

The chocolate had started to melt in the heat.

Changing Air Temperature

The **temperature** of something can be changed by the temperature of the air around it.

When the air around this snowman starts to warm up, the snow will turn to water. The snowman will begin to melt.

(i) *Snow is made of tiny pieces of frozen water.*

See for yourself...

Jonathan's soup was too hot for him to eat, so he left it for awhile.

The colder air around the soup soon cooled the soup down.

Now its temperature is just right!

Cooking

Heat can be used to cook food.

There are lots of different ways to heat food.

It can be boiled in water or fried in oil. It can be baked in the oven or grilled. It can be microwaved or even barbecued.

? *How is your favorite meal cooked?*

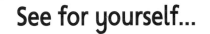

See for yourself...

Alex is eating a potato.
It has been baked in the oven.

Potatoes can be cooked in
many ways. How many
different ways can you
think of?

21

Changes

This chef is making some bread. He is going to bake the **dough** in the oven.

Heat changes the dough from a squishy, stretchy **mixture** into a **solid** loaf of bread.

(i) *When it has been heated, the bread cannot be changed back into squishy dough.*

See for yourself...

Adam is using clay to make a pot.

When he has finished the pot, his mother will bake it in the oven.

Heating the clay changes it from a soft, squishy pot into a hard, dry pot.

Glossary

degrees the units or "steps" that are used to measure temperature

freeze make something so cold that it turns into a **solid**

heating making hotter

liquid something that can be poured

lukewarm cooler than warm but warmer than cool

measure find the amount of something

melt become liquid

mixture anything made by mixing things together

solid something with a shape that stays the same

temperature the heat of something

tepid similar to **lukewarm**

thermometer an object used to measure **temperature**

Index

More Books to Read

Fowler, Allan. *Hot & Cold*. Danbury, Conn.: Children's Press, 1994.

Richardson, Joy. *Heat*. Danbury, Conn.: Franklin Watts, 1994.

24